M000100124

I Am A Disciple

Pastor Chris Brown

Copyright page

Ordering information:

Quantity Sales. Special discounts are available in quantity purchases by corporations, associations, networking groups.

Includes biographical references and index

Dedication

This book exemplifies how my mother and my father, Mr. & Ms. Brown, dedicated their Godly life to raise a God -fearing young man to admire the admonishment of the Lord. I dedicate my book to my local church assembly, Covenant Purpose & Restoration Family Center. Last but not least, I dedicate this book to my children, and most of all my beautiful wife, who is a wonderful woman of God, my Administrator, and Co-Pastor.

Special Thanks

I would like to send a special "Thank You" to my current leaders Apostle Harrison Nichols and Bishop Clinton Richard from the World Outreach Christian Assembly.

I would also like to include a special "Thank You" to the special spiritual leaders I've had throughout my life: Reverend George Pryor of New Birth Baptist Church - Missionary Baptist in Dallas, Bishop NL Hinton of First Apostolic Assembly PAW, Dallas, TX- PAW, Pastor Larry Flenniken of New Life Tabernacle UPCI, in Sherman, TX, Bishop Leon Parker of Zion Apostolic Temple - PAW in Dallas, TX, and the late Pastor Raymond Williams of Bethel Apostolic Church -PAW in Sherman, TX.

Foreword

Discipleship is just like any other vessel; it begins at one point and proceeds to another point. The word disciple, as stated by google search, means to be a disciplined follower, or to agree to the leadership of the person that you're   following.

I read Pastor Chris Brown's book *"I am a Disciple"* before several emotions began crowding my mind. First, I was impressed with the amount of scholarship he employed in developing the manuscript. Next, I was amazed and aspired as I read each example about, he sacrificed and demonstrated what a committed Christian should be about. I had to take a look at my own self and question if indeed I had accepted those values for myself.

Values that inspired me to become disciplined in areas I've never considered before. Every Christian becomes uncomfortable at some point in their life. To walk the easy route and do follow what the world does and call it Christianity is the Western mindset. As I'm witnessing world events where Christians are being killed because they have become disciplined followers, I'm convicted! When I see churches bombed and church members killed in the name and sake of Christ, I think about my ideal Sunday Morning Experience, and to be honest with you, I am ashamed!

How do we justify watered-down Christianity and call it discipleship? Engaged maybe twice a week and call ourselves committed Christians? Of course, the answer is that we cannot. You look around the world, even in poverty-stricken areas, the result is Christians are not standing up and being disciplined. We all should be very ashamed of ourselves.

Chris Brown has written an in your face book that challenges us to look at the man in the mirror and question are you disciplined. Is that how you see your life? I know that I cannot answer truthfully yes, but I will read this book and make the conscious decision to strive to be better. Thank you, Chris, for forcing me to look at myself and realize that I am not all I should be yet.

~Bishop Clinton Richard~

I Am A Disciple

Table of Contents

Contents

Copyright page 3

Dedication 4

Foreword 6

Table of Contents 10

Introduction 11

Who I Am! 15

Chapter 1: The I Am Factor 41

Chapter 2: I am disciplined in my emotions 51

Chapter 3: I Am Disciplined In My Body 67

Chapter 4: I Am Disciplined In Worship 77

Chapter 5: I am Disciplined in Finances 89

Chapter 6: I Am Destined For Greatness 105

About the Author 121

Introduction

1. **Who I Am** - Backstory 1 Corinthians 15:10 King James Version (KJV) 10 *But by the grace of God I am what I am: and His grace which was bestowed upon me was not in vain; but I laboured more abundantly than they all: yet not I, but the grace of God which was with me.*

2. **The I Am Factor** Exodus 3:14 King James Version (KJV) 14 *And God said unto Moses, I Am That I Am: and he said, Thus shalt thou say unto the children of Israel, I Am hath sent me unto you.*

3. I Am Disciplined In My Mind and Emotions Proverbs 4:23 King James Version (KJV)23 *Keep thy heart with all diligence; for out of it are the issues of life.*

4. I Am Disciplined In My Body/Health & Wellness 1 Peter 2:24 King James Version (KJV) 24 *Who his own self bare our sins in His own body on the tree, that we, being dead to sins, should live unto righteousness: by whose stripes ye were healed.*

5. I Am Disciplined In My Spirituality – Worship/Faith Matthew 16:24 *Then Jesus said unto His disciples, "If any man will come after Me, let him deny himself and take up his cross and follow Me.*

6. **I am Disciplined in my Finances - Stewardship** 1 Corinthians 4:2 King James Version (KJV) 2 *Moreover it is required in stewards, that a man be found faithful.*

7. **I Am Destined For Greatness** Romans 8:29-30 King James Version (KJV) 29 *For whom he did foreknow, he also did predestinate to be conformed to the image of his Son, that he might be the firstborn among many brethren. 30 Moreover whom he did predestinate, them he also called: and whom he called, them he also justified: and whom he justified, them he also glorified.*

Who I Am!

Good morning, good afternoon, and good evening to all my readers. We will endeavor to look at the life of a believer who is adamant in declaring: I am a disciple!

My name is Pastor Chris Brown and many years ago I made the decided to "follow Jesus all the way". As the old saints used to sing growing up in a little Pentecostal church. "I made a vow unto the Lord that I won't turn back. I'm down on my knees making a holy vow that I won't turn back." This is the life and a story of a Christian disciple who has had many trials, tribulations, setbacks, heartbreaks and disappointments. Nevertheless, I made a promise unto the Lord that I would not turn back.

I was born in Dallas, Texas, in 1975, to my lovely mother, Mrs. Brown. I truly thank God that he gave me a praying mother. Through many of my life hardships, my mother has always been a prayer intercessor on my behalf. She continues to be married to my wonderful father, Mr. Brown, for over 30 years now and they both have been an inspiration in my life for many years. I gave my life unto the Lord at the young tender age of eight years old on June 6, 1983. I received the baptism of the Holy Spirit on January 27, 1984. Then I was later baptized in the wonderful name of Jesus Christ.

Though I was full of zeal at this young age, I still lacked knowledge in my relationship with Jesus Christ. Even though my mother and father we're of different denominations, I learned from them both. My dad being Baptist, I learned systematic theology and my mom being Apostolic Pentecostal, I learned spontaneous worship and praise.

Many times, I've found in religion that we are going back-and-forth over Christian dogmas and -isms and schisms in the Christian faith. However, I've concluded that we have more on which to agree than to disagree. The Bible teaches us that wise is he that winneth a soul.

In being a disciple, I have learned that people want to know that you care before they care what you know. Thus, I have learned to show love to people in a more compassionate and caring way. In following the example of Christ, I must show them that I care and that I genuinely love them in the way that God has commanded us to love. So, in deciding to be a disciple of Christ, I have decided to let love be my religion. Above all else, he has commanded us to love Him and to love our neighbors as we love ourselves. I ask you as a disciple of Christ, in the words of a Jamaican singer, "So now that we found love what are we going to do with it?"

Jesus commands us to go and make disciples of men. Beloved, we do this by showing the world love. From a young child to an adolescent teen and up to my adult years, the process of me becoming a disciple took place during the time of my family relocating from the urban city of Dallas, TX, to a small country town north of Dallas named Sherman, TX.

Looking back, those were indeed my defining years. It was during this time where I begin to give my testimonies within the church. It was because of the spiritual connections during these years that I grew to be able to say, "I Am A Disciple." As a young teen, I made up in my mind to let Jesus be my best friend, and if I had no other friends in school, I knew that if I had Jesus, that was enough. All throughout my junior high and high school years, my peers respected me for being a disciple of Christ. While living in Sherman, I went to a church that was comprised of mostly Caucasian brothers and sisters. Nevertheless, I was welcomed by the pastor and his wife. I will never forget them and the love and compassion they showed me.

It was in the transition of coming from a predominately black church in the inner city and then worshiping with brethren of another color that I learned that people are people no matter the color of their skin. Even in the church, you have good and bad, kind and mean, loving, and hateful people. In other words, you will have both wheat and tares growing together, but Jesus says, let them grow together, and in the end, He would divide them.

While worshipping in our small church in Sherman, I learned to love people who did not look like me or think like me. The process of learning to love diverse people made me who I am today. Loving without prejudice, racism, or bigotry, but learning to embrace who I am as a disciple and love people regardless of who they are as an essential part of that process. I accepted the call of God to ministry at age 16 and was tutored by a great pastor who taught me to be a people person and to love all people.

The Apostle Paul put it this way, I become everything to everybody that I may win a soul. *FYI ~ A message to the young people you don't have to fall into sin so you can have a testimony, but your evidence can be that God kept you and you didn't fall.*

I've learned that the same grace that can pick you up from a fall is the same grace that can keep you from falling. I was an eager young minister in the making; however, I would never forget what a prophetess told me in a prayer meeting at a family member's house when I was young. She prophesied that I would go through a lot of heartbreak and heartache and that I would fall and make some mistakes along my road to Christian discipleship, but she told me not to worry that

God was going to use all of that to make me who I am, a disciple.

Also, she said after going through these things I would be able to minister unto people with not just sympathy but empathy. I would be able to look at people not with eyes of judgment and condemnation, but literally, be able to look at them through the eyes of God. She said that I would be able to see them with eyes of agape love. Agape love can be defined as unconditional love for people. As I got older, the prophecy that I received at a young age slowly came to pass.

At the age of 20, I thought it was the right decision at the time. I got married. The conclusion that I made to get married was my choice, but looking back, it was not God's choice. I ignored the voice of God, the sound of reasoning, the voice of warning and decided to do what I wanted. This decision forever changed the course of my life. I would never be the same again.

My ex-wife, and I were young and did not fully understand the seriousness of the marriage vows. We later ended up in divorce court because of irreconcilable differences. Two children the marriage and a divorce which is an ugly word, destroys everyone involved.

While I was going through my divorce, I physically felt like someone was ripping me apart on the inside. It was one of the worst feelings I have ever experienced. It is a feeling I would not wish on my worst enemy. The Bible says flesh of my flesh and bone of my bone, and it literally felt like my flesh and bones where being torn apart. Before I finally decided to proceed with the divorce, I tried to stay and tough it out.

Unfortunately, I learned the hard way that anything that is not God-ordained will not last. When we have made decisions that are contrary to the will of God for our lives, we must allow God to intervene in our lives to correct those decisions. So, with much prayer, confirmation, and consideration, we divorced.

I felt like the divorce wounded me spiritually, emotionally, mentally, and financially. While going through this life-changing event, I felt like there was no one I could talk to that would understand what I was going through. The Bible says in the multitude of counselors, there is safety, and that love covers a multitude of sins. Unfortunately, I had no counselors and was out of the covering of God.

This divorce caused me to have feelings of shame, guilt, worry, and condemnation. Voices were voices running through my head that I knew were not of God. I was disappointed in myself for making such a horrible decision. I did not know how I would ever recover from such a low point. Loneliness and contemplation of suicide made me want to give up on God and life because of my poor decision.

I just felt defeated. It was during this time that I should have reached out to the elders of the church and tried to seek counseling. It is a trick of the devil to cause us to feel alone and isolated. It is during this time that I sunk deeper into loneliness and depression. Warning always comes before destruction, but oftentimes we do not heed the voice of God. I was not heeding God's voice, which drastically altered the course of my life.

During this time, I became someone my mother did not raise me to be. I began to live a life of sin and worldliness. I tried to fill the void and pain inside by trying to self-medicate with sexual promiscuity, drugs, and alcohol. Later, I comprehended that it only made me worse and not better. These things only left me bitter, not better.

My life was taking a downward spiral into a life of hell. Thankfully, even during those times I remembered that God was still with me. In the Psalms, David writes, "If I ascend into heaven, thou art there; if I make my bed in hell, behold, thou art there." The call of God never left me, even in my foolishness, and for that, I am ever grateful. God kept me even when I did not deserve to be kept. The Bible says gifts and callings are without repentance. I remember the time my mother prayed for me before I went to a party. She asked me, ***"Son, do you believe God can hear a sinner's prayer?"***

That made me realize that my present situation was a mess. I was living a life of living in sin and degradation. I thought to myself that if I was honest with God, then sincerely, he could hear a sinner's prayer.

After telling my mom I believed and that she could pray for me, she proceeded to pray.

She intensely began to pray for me like a tongue talking Apostolic woman of God. I got nervous because it was killing my wanting to party vibe.

I am so glad God gave me a praying mother! I went ahead to go to the party. At the party, I met all my friends, and we begin to drink and party. We were all hanging together outside at an apartment complex. When suddenly, a drug dealer came out of nowhere and pulled out a gun. Everybody cleared out except me. I had my back turned to him and never saw him coming. Suddenly, in my intoxicated state, I realized that everybody was gone except me.

I turned around to see a man pointing a gun in my direction and screaming and yelling. I knew the guy, and I had my hands lifted to the sky and speaking to him in reference to his accusations. I told him that whatever his problem was that it wasn't me. So, he jumped in his car and sped off.

Saints, I know it was the blood for me! One day when I was lost, Jesus died upon that cross. I know it was the blood for me!

My mother's intercessory prayers had covered me! All during the process of the making of my testimony, God's hands were on me. Even when I thought I was outside of His covering, I never was. God was always protecting and covering me. While selling drugs and partying, the hand of the Lord was still on me. So finally, God said my time of sin was up and that He was looking for "Yes Lord" from me. I felt God tricked me in how he got me back into fellowship with Him.

The same thing that led me away from God was the same thing He used to get me back in fellowship with Him. **A woman**. This young lady I was dating at the time knew I was running the streets and living a riotous lifestyle, but she found my weak spot in my heart and got me to open, about my life.

The greatest weakness, but strength to me is (1) talking about my Lord and Savior Jesus Christ and (2) talking about my children. Those two subjects are my vulnerability, and she figured it out. So, in the process, I started to go back to church again. But while going back, I was still trying to play so hard. I did not want to clap my hands, worship, or anything. Every time I kept coming to church and sitting in the worship service, it felt like the fire of the Holy Ghost was steadily breaking me on down.

So eventually, I begin to hear the voice of God again in my life, telling me that the curse had been broken off my life. The time of illicit activity and partying was over. Also, the Holy Spirit told me one morning that I was going to go back to praying like I used to. Not knowing later that day, I was set up by the Holy Ghost in such a way that it caused me to fulfill the word of the Lord, which He had spoken to me.

At the time, I was talking to a young lady, and her uncle was in serious need of prayer. So, they called me to come over and pray. When I went to pray, I ran into a man that was under the influence of drugs and alcohol. He was about to go crazy, and they asked me to help pray - the backslidden sinner. I did not know what to do, but I felt like I did not need to get involved.

However, because they asked for my help and did not want to call the authorities, I stepped in. In Jesus' Name, I took a breath and looked right at the man who was charging at me and growling. I opened my mouth and *said Satan, I rebuke you in Jesus' Name.*

The power and authority showed up at the mention of His name, which made the devil behave. This man who over 300-pounds and charging towards me to attack me fell to the ground just like when David slew Goliath. The word of the Lord was fulfilled. I eventually had to let go of the world and get back into Zion.

I stopped doing everything that was not pleasing to God or that which was not becoming of a Christian. God started to do some major restoration work on me. Once I got back in covenant with God, He began to reveal to me my purpose and direct my life. I eventually got remarried and got back to working in the church.

I am that I am by the grace of God! Finally, I came to a surrendering part in my life that I begin to get reconnected with my savior Jesus Christ! It was at that point I began to renew my vows to the Lord and believe in my heart and confess with my mouth the Lord

Jesus. That's when he saved me from myself and covered me.

A disciple of Christ is one who is a disciplined follower! We as Christians have decided to follow Jesus, no turning back, no turning back. My prayer is that in you reading this book, you will make that decision not only to be a Christian but that you will become a disciple of Christ.

I Am A Disciple

The Bible says life and death is in the power of the tongue. The world calls this principle of speaking forth into the atmosphere the law of attraction, but we the people of God we call this principle of the word prayer and faith.

Pastor Chris Brown

Chapter 1: The I Am Factor

T he I am factor is a powerful confirmation and affirmation statement to use in any situation, whether good or bad, you decide.

The Bible says life and death are in the power of the tongue. The world calls this principle of speaking forth into the atmosphere the law of attraction, but we, the people of God we call this principle of the word prayer and faith.

There is nothing new under the sun. The same God right now is the same God that existed back then. I once heard Bishop Tudor Bismark say, *"Every time you use the "I am factor, it is for a memorial in the earth in reverence to the name of God. Everything you say after I am becomes in existence. So let the weak say I am strong. Let the poor say I am rich."*

God told Moses to tell pharaoh the I Am that I Am sent you. God will be whatever you need him to be in any situation. No matter what is going on in your life, I believe you must decree and declare a powerful affirmation of speaking forth those things that are not as though they were.

We, as believers, know that we walk by faith and not by sight. As the late Bishop Norman L. Wagner said: *"We are spiritual beings living in this earthly realm."* Hebrews 11:1-6 King James Version (KJV) *1 Now faith is the substance of things hoped for, the evidence of things not seen. 2 For by it, the elders obtained a good report. 3 Through faith we understand that the world was framed by the word of God so that things which are seen were not made of things which do appear. 4 By faith, Abel offered unto God a more excellent sacrifice than Cain, by which he obtained witness that he was righteous, God testifying of his gifts: and by it, he is being dead yet speaketh. 5 By faith Enoch was translated that he should not see death; and was not found, because God had translated him: for before his translation he had this testimony, that he pleased God. 6 But without faith, it is impossible to please him: for he that cometh to God must believe that he is, and that he, is a rewarder of them that diligently seek him.*

Beloved, we must remain diligent in the faith, which requires both speaking and moving in the word of God. All that we need is in the word of God. For every situation in life, the Bible provides an answer. While on the road back to the right relationship with God, I had to speak life back into my situation with numerous confirmations and affirmations of his Holy Word. The most important thing I've spoken over my life is one confirmation that is the anchor for my soul.

No matter what's going on in my life, good or bad, I've learned to say, *"I AM A DISCIPLE!!!"* I'm not just a Christian. I'm not just a Fan. I'm not just a fair-weather saint. I AM A DISCIPLE of Jesus Christ. He is my Lord and King! I owe him my life because he gave his life for me over 2000 years ago.

Over the next chapters, we will endeavor to see how and what it really means to say that you are a disciple of Jesus Christ! Then Jesus said unto His disciples, *"If any man will come after Me, let him deny himself and take up his cross and follow Me."* Being a real disciple of Christ will require discipline in every aspect of your life! We live in a post-modernist Christian age where people feel they can do whatever they want and still proclaim Jesus. God forbids!

The Buddhists, Hinduists, and Islamists have life discipline, but the people of *"in God, we Trust"* are allowing our God to be our belly. What can we consume more upon our flesh instead of living in the spirit? It's time to be awakened and not let Satan have an advantage over us through the lust of our flesh. In this Christian journey, it is not a lack of God's power but a lack of our discipline, which causes much of our suffering.

A lot of us suffer spiritually, financially, emotionally, mentally, and socially, because of a lack of discipline. It's not a lack of the word of God, the anointing, or the power of God, only a lack of our discipline. If we are going to be real disciples, we must understand that we need discipline. I am a disciplined follower of Jesus Christ - we must speak and live those words.

Through good days, bad days, through sickness and in health, rich or poor, up or down, happy or sad, I will follow Him. The old hymn said, "I have decided to follow Jesus. No turning back, no turning back." In this Laodicean age, we must understand that there is no lack of God's power for our healing and deliverance. The only lack is on our part. We lack in giving of ourselves totally wholeheartedly to the savior body, mind, soul, and money! To be a disciple, you must be willing to love him with all your heart, mind, soul and body.

I Am A Disciple

What is your "I Am" Affirmation?

_____

_____

Think of a time that you have used your "I Am" to define your Moment

_____

_____

What Best Describes your "I Am" Mindset?

The human heart brings about so much complexity at times that it could cause one to go crazy in the mind. The things of our past the hurts, the wounds, the abuse, the neglect, the anxiety, the heart break, loneliness, depression, all because of an heart that is overwhelmed with life issues.

Pastor Chris Brown

Chapter 2: I Am Disciplined In My Emotions

In the word of the Lord, we understand that the mind and human emotions will play a big part of being a disciple. The Bible says as a man thinketh so is he! I present to you that the three social realities of our society are psychology, philosophy, and religion.

The one thing that bridges them all together is that they all agree on one the truth; we become what we think! From the biblical perspective, we understand that in the scriptures, when the word "mind" is used, it is referencing our intellectual conceptualization of the word.

However, when you see the word "heart" in the scriptures, it is dealing with our human emotions. So now the Bible says in Philippians 2:5-11 King James Version (KJV) *5 Let this mind be in you, which was also in Christ Jesus: 6 Who, being in the form of God, thought it not robbery to be equal with God: 7 But made himself of no reputation, and took upon him the form of a servant, and was made in the likeness of men: 8 And being found in fashion as a man, he humbled himself, and became obedient unto death, even the death of the cross.*

Just like Jesus showed us the discipline of the mind by humbling himself to God, we need the heart to follow through with the Word of God. The Greek word "*logos* "translates to the thought, idea, or plan of God. We can have all of God's word in our mind, but if it doesn't get in our heart, it becomes of no effect.

To fulfill God's word, the heart must be applied. There will be trying times, but Romans 8:28 King James Version (KJV) lets us know that: *And we know that all things work together for good to them that love God, to them who are the called according to his purpose.*

Even when Jesus was in the Garden of Gethsemane, he wrestled in his mind with "the plan". He knew full well the truth was that he had to go to the cross, but his heart wasn't ready yet. It was only when He said in Matthew 26:39 King James Version (KJV) 39, *And he went a little farther, and fell on his face, and prayed, saying, O my Father, if it be possible, let this cup pass from me: nevertheless not as I will, but as thou wilt that he was ready to go forth and do the will of God.*

The surrendering of the heart: the will and emotions are essential to be a disciplined follower. Therefore, the psalmist says *thy word have I hid in my heart, not the mind that I might not sin against thee.* It's only when we surrender our hearts that we can be obedient to God.

So, with a heart full of the Love of God, we can keep his commandments! We love him because he first loved us by suffering, bleeding, and dying for us. God doesn't care about how much of the Word you can quote, but rather how much of the Word you live daily? *Selah*!

The human heart brings about so much complexity at times that it could cause one to go crazy at times. The things of our past including the hurts, the wounds, the abuse, the neglect, the anxiety, the heartbreak, the loneliness, and the depression, are all symptoms heart that is overwhelmed with life issues.

No wonder the psalmist says **when my heart is overwhelmed lead me to the rock that's higher than I.** It's only in prayer that we can have an outlet for all these sick and intoxicating emotions that would try to destroy us and cause us to have an emotional breakdown. God is faithful, and He is our

"Rock". He is the One that can stabilize our heart and our emotions when everything is going crazy all around us. Isaiah 26:3 King James Version (KJV) 3 *Thou wilt keep him in perfect peace, whose mind is stayed on thee: because he trusteth in thee.*

We must discipline ourselves with daily consumptions of the word. Simply put, if you want to have peace in your life, your mind must stay on Him. A steady consumption of the word helps to keep you strong and your mind stays on Him.

When thinking about the disciplining of the mind, I think of the great quote. *"A mind is a terrible thing to waste"* Here lies familiar passages of scriptures Romans Chapter 7: 15-25 in which it depicts this epic generational universal struggle of the mind & will, the emotions of the heart toward God- struggling with good and evil. Verses 15-21 lets us know that the struggle is real.

Every day the struggle is real, yet, we have the power of choice of whether to do good or to do evil. These scriptures are the conclusion on the matter of discipline of the mind. Romans 7:22-25 King James Version (KJV) *22 For I delight in the law of God after the inward man: 23 But I see another law in my members, warring against the law of my mind, and bringing me into captivity to the law of sin which is in my members. 24 O wretched man that I am! Who shall deliver me from the body of this death? 25 I thank God through Jesus Christ, our Lord. So then with the mind, I myself serve the law of God, but with the flesh the law of sin.*

The apostle says in vs. 23, I see another law warring against the law of mind! These passages of scriptures vs. 15-23 are dealing with what psychology defines as "cognitive dissonance ". Cognitive dissonance is defined as the state of having inconsistent thoughts, beliefs, or attitudes, especially as relating to behavioral decisions and attitude change. Verse 19 states, *so well for the good that I would I do not: but the evil which I would not, that I do.* Herein lies a problem with the discipline of the mind. Some of us are struggling with what psychologist's call "predispositions". Predisposition can be defined as a liability or tendency to suffer from a condition, hold a specific attitude, or act in a particular way.

Our minds have been conditioned by childhood upbringings, family customs, traditions, deprived communities, and some generational curses. All our life experiences shape who we grow to be. The psalmist writes of this conditioning in Psalm 51:5 King James Version (KJV) 5 *Behold, I was sharpened in iniquity; and in sin did my mother conceive me.*

Life has a way of programming our minds. For instance, the movie called "The Matrix," Mr. Anderson had to learn how to become unplugged from his current surroundings called 'The Matrix" and went into another place outside of time. In other words, to become a true disciple, we have to become unattached to this world and learn to get plugged into the word of God to get the victory over the lust of the flesh, lust of the eyes, and pride of life.

List some ways to be Disciplined in your mind:

_____
_____
_____
_____
_____
_____
_____

List ways you can be Disciplined in your emotions:

_____
_____
_____
_____
_____
_____
_____
_____

What are some benefits of a disciplined mind?

_____
_____
_____
_____
_____
_____

What are some issues of an undisciplined mind?

_____
_____
_____
_____
_____
_____

What are some steps you can take to Discipline your Emotions?

_____
_____
_____
_____
_____
_____
_____
_

What are some problems from having an undisciplined emotional makeup:_____

_____
_____
_____
_____
_____
_____

9 I Am Disciplined in my Mind & Emotions

Affirmations:

1:

2:

3:

4:

5:

6:

7:

8:

9:

I Am A Disciple

Behind every miracle there are instructions. God can use the doctor and the medicine to heal us, but we have to do our part with being disciplined in our bodies. That's the truth! There's no need to come through the prayer line if you are not going to change your ways and lifestyles of eating and living. The Bible says faith without works is dead. If we do our part and God will do his part.

Pastor Chris Brown

Chapter 3: I Am Disciplined In My Body

I Am Disciplined In My Body/Health & Wellness. ***"The brain and peripheral nervous system, the endocrine and immune systems, and indeed, all the organs of our body and all the emotional responses we have, share a common chemical language and are constantly communicating with one another."*** Quote from Dr. James Gordon (founder of the Center for Mind-Body Medicine).

Our bodies dictate our brains how and what we feel. So, a lot of the time, the way we feel is dictated by the health & wellness of our bodies. Think for a moment. God never intended for man to die, but because of sin entering the world by the first Adam, sin brought about sickness and disease and eventually the body dying and decaying.

Men in the Old Testament lived for hundreds of years. It was a different ecosystem, and they had more of a plant-based diet. God designed the human body to recover itself from injury through the workings of white blood cells. White blood cells are our bodies' mechanisms to fight off sickness & diseases in our bodies.

God already strategically engineered our body to heal itself. Taking proper care of ourselves assists our bodies in the healing process. We can take good care of our bodies by getting proper rest, diet, exercise, and meditation on the word of God. The Bible says in 1 Corinthians 6:19-20 (KJV) 19 ***What? know ye not that your body is the temple of the Holy Ghost, which is in you, which ye have of God, and ye are not your own? 20 For ye are bought with a price: therefore, glorify God in your body, and in your spirit, which are God's.***

Many of our mental & emotional problems are a derivative of poor health &

wellness. God designed our bodies to heal themselves. Think about that! I personally had some health issues present themselves in 2018, and God put it in my spirit that if I did my part, He would do his part.

Behind every miracle, there are instructions. God can use doctors and their medicine to heal us, but we must do our part with being disciplined in our choices about what we put into our bodies. That's the truth! There's no need to come through the prayer line if you are not going to change your ways and lifestyles of eating and living. The Bible says faith without works is dead. If we do our part, God will do his part.

So many believers are leaving this world before time, not due to aging and natural causes, but because of the lack of a disciplined and healthy lifestyles. It's high time that we become disciplined saints. So, in my personal health issues, I thank God for healing, changing my diet and lifestyle, restoring my health, and I believe he can do the same for you as well.

When the body seems to get, weak remember that by his stripes that he bore on his own body we are healed. The blood in the natural body, is designed to regenerate. How much more *"THE BLOOD OF JESUS!!!!"* will always prevail.

Just a reminder beloved, when saints die, the sickness and disease are not what caused their death. God, in His infinite wisdom, decided that it was their time. We must remember that to live is Christ and die gain. In closing, when talking about health and wellness, we not only need the word of God to recover spiritually, but sometimes an excellent physical exercise program helps in your daily practical road to recovery as well. I believe God can heal miraculously, and he can also improve us through a daily process of instructions for healing.

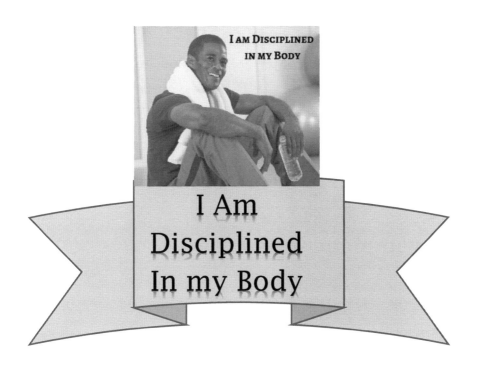

I Am
Disciplined
In my Body

5 Key ways to become disciplined in your

Body:

1

2

3

4

5

4 reasons why your health is important?

1

2

3

4

3 reasons why Wellness Matters

1:

2:

3:

2 Things you can do today to improve your health

1:

2:

1 Things to do to improve your Health

1:

We have to have that determination and commitment to continue in faith. Sometimes we might fall or make some mistakes, but we have to keep moving forward in faith. Our worship demands total submission to God. In order to do His will we have to be sold out completely at whatever cost.

Pastor Chris Brown

Chapter 4: I Am Disciplined In Worship

The Bible says in John 4:24 King James Version (KJV) 24 *God is a Spirit: and they that worship him must worship him in spirit and in truth.* The devil is a spirit, but he isn't the truth. For the Bible says he is the father of lies and truth is not in him. The truth of the word of God is the vital point to keep us on track in following God which is a part of being a disciple of Christ.

Jesus said I am the way the truth and the life no man come to the father but by me. Now that we have the truth, we must be willing to follow Jesus all the way home. Hebrews 11:6 *says* **but without faith it is impossible to please him: for he that cometh to God must believe that he is, and that he is a rewarder of them that diligently seek him.**

We must have that determination and commitment to continue in faith. Sometimes we might fall or make some mistakes, but we must keep moving forward in faith. True worship demands total submission to God. In order to do his will, we must be sold out completely at whatever cost.

Discipleship will cost you your whole life just like Jesus gave His life. He gave His life so that we could have eternal life. He desires our life so He can live through us to reach the masses. Our faith must be disciplined in the word of God to the point that we only believe God and have no doubt. Belief in God is quintessential to pure Worship. Hebrews 11:6 says *but without faith it is impossible to please Him. For he that cometh to God must believe that He is, and that He is a rewarder of them that diligently seek Him.*

We must stand on the promises of God. His Word says that He can do it and we must believe that if His words says that He can do it that He will do it. Worship is a part of being a disciple. Just like Abraham said in Genesis

22:*5 And Abraham said unto his young men, Abide ye here with the ass; and I and the lad will go yonder and worship, and come again to you.*

Worship will always require a sacrifice. Pure worship requires you to become submissive just like Isaac and present yourself on the altar as a living sacrifice. In today's world submissiveness and humility is not looked upon with honor. Even though being submissive and humble is not popular it is required, you cannot go to a higher place in God called "worship" until you are ready to humbly and submissively yield yourself to him totally. Romans 12:1 *says I beseech you therefore, brethren, by the mercies of God, that ye present your bodies a living sacrifice, holy, acceptable unto God, which is your reasonable service.*

So, we must understand there is a difference in being religious and being spiritual. The Bible tells us that the Pharisees and the Sadducees were a strict and pious religious sect of that day, but they were not so spiritual as Jesus tells us. Jesus says that they looked holy and pure on the outside, but inside they were full of dead men's bones. They had a zeal for God but lacked knowledge.

In order to be spiritual, it must start on the inside. The spiritual aspects of life require much prayer and fasting. When struggling with things of our past and trying to let go of past hurts and past wounds, bad habits, and addictions we need much prayer & fasting. Prayer & Fasting are our weapons to defeat the enemies of our flesh and spirit that war against our souls and keep us from pure worship. Jesus said in Matthew 17:21 ***Howbeit this kind goeth not out but by prayer and fasting.***

Is there anything too hard for the Lord? No, I don't think so. Prayer and fasting mixed with faith will remove those hindrances out of your life. I'm a witness. 2 Corinthians 10:4-5 Says *4 (For the weapons of our warfare are not carnal, but mighty through God to the pulling down of strongholds;) 5 Casting down imaginations, and every high thing that exalteth itself against the knowledge of God, and bringing into captivity every thought to the obedience of Christ.* Also, Ephesians 6:12 King James Version (KJV) 12 *For we wrestle not against flesh and blood, but against principalities, against powers, against the rulers of the darkness of this world, against spiritual wickedness in high places.*

The Christian struggle is not natural warfare, but a spiritual one. Therefore, we must learn to discipline ourselves spiritually.

I Am A Disciple

List some ways to be Disciplined in your worship:

_____
_____
_____
_____
_____
_____
_____

List ways you can be Disciplined in your emotions:

_____
_____
_____
_____
_____
_____
_____
_____

What are some benefits of disciplined

worship?

_____
_____
_____
_____
_____

I Am A Disciple

What are some issues of undisciplined worship?

_____
_____
_____
_____
_____
_____

What are some steps you can take to become more Disciplined your worship?

_____
_____
_____
_____
_____
_____
_____
_

What are some problems of having an undisciplined worship life?

:_____
_____
_____
_____
_____
_____
_____

86 | P a g e

9 I Am Disciplined in my Mind & Emotions

Affirmations:

1:

2:

3:

4:

5:

6:

7:

8:

9:

Our family belongs to God. Our money, our wife, our husband, our friends, our churches, our children, our money, our bodies and our lives all belong to God. I've heard some great theologians say so with this revelation in mind we must wear our life in this world like a loose garment knowing we can't take anything with us as my Egyptian brothers in past attempted to do. You can not take a U-haul to grave with you.

Chris Brown

Chapter 5: I am Disciplined in Finances

The Bible says in Malachi 3:8-18 *8 Will a man rob God? Yet ye have robbed me. But ye say, Wherein have we robbed thee? In tithes and offerings. 9 Ye are cursed with a curse: for ye have robbed me, even this whole nation. 10 Bring ye all the tithes into the storehouse, that there may be meat in mine house, and prove me now herewith, saith the Lord of hosts, if I will not open you the windows of heaven, and pour you out a blessing, that there shall not be room enough to receive it. 11 And I will rebuke the*

devourer for your sakes, and he shall not destroy the fruits of your ground; neither shall your vine cast her fruit before the time in the field, saith the Lord of hosts. 12 And all nations shall call you blessed: for ye shall be a delightsome land, saith the Lord of hosts.

I do not believe in a fear-based theology of trying to manipulate scriptures to force or try to control people to do what God has already commanded they do. I believe in speaking the word and letting God do the rest. With that being said, the Bible says it rains on the just as well as the unjust. Ecclesiastes 9:11 Solomon *says I returned and saw under the sun, that the race is not to the swift, nor the battle to the strong, neither yet bread to the wise, nor yet riches to men of understanding, nor yet favour to men of skill; but time and chance happeneth to them all.*

The Bible shows us that God gives man dominion over the earth in Genesis and told him to be fruitful & multiply. I believe God is a God of progression and harvest. Herein lies the answer Genesis 8:22 says *While the earth remaineth, seedtime and harvest, and cold and heat, and summer and winter, and day and night shall not cease.*

Before any harvest we must sow seeds. You cannot reap where you have not sown. God hates bareness and emptiness. Remember the story where Jesus curses the fig tree for not having fruit? What about the story of the man with the talent that hid it in the ground in Matthew 25:25-27 says *And I was afraid, and went and hid thy talent in the earth: lo, there thou hast that is thine. His lord answered and said unto him, Thou wicked and slothful servant, thou knewest that I reap where I sowed not, and gather where I have not strawed: Thou oughtest therefore to have put my money to the exchangers, and then at my coming I should have received mine own with usury.* <u>Clearly God is serious about being fruitful and multiplying. He has not given us talents, gifts and blessings for us to waste them.</u>

Galatians 6:7-9 says *be not deceived; God is not mocked: for whatsoever a man soweth, that shall he also reap.* This Biblical principle is true in every aspect of our spiritual life.

The Bible says 1 Corinthians 4:1-2 *Let a man so account of us, as of the ministers of Christ, and stewards of the mysteries of God. Moreover, it is required in stewards, that a man be found faithful.* God has set us over all that is His in the earth. The Bible says that the earth is the Lord's, and the fullness thereof; the world, and they that dwell therein. We must understand beloved that everything belongs to God, He just allows us to be overseers of His property.

Our family belongs to God, our money, our wife, our husband, our friends, our churches, our children, our money our bodies and our lives all belong to God. I've heard some great theologians say so with this revelation in mind we must wear our life in this world like a loose garment knowing we cannot take anything with us as my Egyptian brothers in past attempted to do. You cannot take a U-haul to the grave with you.

So, with this understanding, the Bible says in Matthew 6:21 ***For where your treasure is, there will your heart be also.*** Ask yourself where do you spend your money the most? The answer will show you where your heart is. When the Israelites were coming out of slavery, they took the gold that they got from Egypt and squandered it all on a golden calf. The reason is that they had an old-worldly mindset of slavery and poverty. Therefore, discipline is so important. We must become free from the old mindsets that have had us bound.

Think about it. Your money can not literally save you spiritually. So why are we so emotional about our money? The Bible says the love of money is the root of all evil. It did not say having money is evil. Malachi teaches us spiritual financial principles in that if we touch not the Holy Thing, "The Tithe", and give God what is due to Him. He would bless us abundantly. Discipline yourself to give God what belongs to him, your first fruit, and I'm a witness He will bless your house.

The tithe is to further the work of the Lords House. It is good ground to sow your seed and you cannot out beat God's giving. The tithe teaches financial discipline over money. After you give God what's his, apply this principle to your own life. You pay all your bills and everybody, but you do not put back anything for yourself. This is a surefire way to remain impoverished.

I was with a friend one Saturday afternoon riding and looking at several of his properties. We arrived at one of his properties that had a pecan tree growing in a garden. We saw a squirrel running around with a nut in his mouth. Then my friend said something to me that was like an epiphany. He said *"that ole squirrel that is getting ready for winter. He went and planted that pecan in the ground to save up for the winter season and forgot that he planted it there."* The thought that a huge tree had taken root from the simple act of a squirrel planting a nut blew me away. Wow! I said to myself. What if people took that same concept and applied it to their finances. What a grand harvest they would have. Instead of eating and consuming all the money we get, we should put something back for a change of season. Then you will be established in all seasons.

Remember the story of the famine in Egypt when Joseph said to put back a portion during the plentiful times so that you would have something in lean times? This principle is still timely and relevant today. My father always told me get to some insurance, so you don't have to be a burden on your family after you are gone. Proverbs 13:22 King James Version (KJV) 22 *A good man leaveth an inheritance to his children's children: and the wealth of the sinner is laid up for the just.* We have a lot of work to do for God and that work takes money and investments to get it accomplished. We must be disciplined in stewardship for our families and the people of God.

List some ways to be Disciplined in your mind:

_____
_____
_____
_____
_____
_____
_____

List ways you can be Disciplined in your finances:

_____
_____
_____
_____
_____
_____
_____
_____
_____

What are some benefits of financial

discipline?

_____
_____
_____
_____
_____

What are some issues of undisciplined
finances?

_____
_____
_____
_____
_____

What are some steps you can take to be Disciplined in your finances?

_____
_____
_____
_____
_____
_____
_____
_

What are some problems from having an undisciplined

f_____
_____
_____
_____
_____
_____

9 I Am Disciplined in my finances

Affirmations:

1:

2:

3:

4:

5:

6:

7:

8:

9:

I Am A Disciple

We were created for greatness in this and the afterlife. No wonder why the Apostle Paul gets the revelation that to live is Christ and die is gain. We can't lose with Jesus being our Savior, because he triumphed over death, grave and hell. One day in prayer I asked the Holy Spirit for a word that would revolutionize my whole way of thinking about life. I heard him tell me that we I have already won.

Pastor Chris Brown

Chapter 6: I Am Destined For Greatness

I am sure everybody has heard brother Jonathan Nelson's song, My Name is Victory. Have you ever just stopped and listened to the words of that song? *"My Name Is Victory" "I've got evidence I've got confidence. I'm a conqueror I know that I win I know who I am. God wrote it in his plan for me Ooh, oh oh my name is VICTORY!*

God gave me authority to conquer the enemy. He wrote in my destiny that my name is victory. He said that I've overcome I know I've already won. He wrote in my destiny that my name is Victory. I know who I am God wrote it in his plan for me. Ooh, oh oh my name is VICTORY! "

It is such a powerful song, and it is true for the believers. The Bible tells us how our story will end in Revelation 12: 10-11 *And I heard a loud voice saying in heaven, Now is come salvation, and strength, and the kingdom of our God, and the power of his Christ: for the accuser of our brethren is cast down, which accused them before our God day and night. 11 And they overcame him by the blood of the Lamb, and by the word of their testimony, and they loved not their lives unto the death.*

We were created for greatness in this life and the afterlife. No wonder why the Apostle Paul gets the revelation that to live is Christ and die is gain. We can't lose with Jesus being our Savior, because he triumphed over death, grave and hell. One day in prayer I asked the Holy Spirit for a word that would revolutionize my whole way of thinking about life. I heard him tell me that I have already won. This revolutionized my entire thought process.

As Jekalyn Carr says *It's already done. Jesus has already won the victory for us. I am not perfect, but I am forgiven. I have been hurt but I am healed. I have been weak, but I am strong I have been poor, but I am rich.* So, I asked God if I have already won what's the purpose for all these life struggles. Then the Holy Spirit gently told me that he uses the circumstances to keep me humble and bring me closer to Him so that I might know Him.

How would you know him as a healer if you were never sick? How would you know him as a way maker if you never had any closed doors and etc.... He told Paul for my grace is enough for thee. For in your weakness my strength is being perfected in you. We must learn to let God be our strength. Remember, the same grace that picks you up after a fall is the same grace that can keep you from a fall. The same Grace given by the I Am.

For when we are truly living by the grace of God every day what keeps going up just keeps going up by the grace of God. He did not set us up for failure, but greatness which is inside all of us. No wonder the writer said greater is He that is in us than He that is in the world.

Which brings us to the conclusion he knew us before we were formed in our mother's womb. He knew every sin, failure, mistakes, bad habits, addictions that we would ever have. Also, don't forget the heartaches and heartbreaks anxiety, stress, worry, low self-esteem we would ever have, He knew them all! Yet he still called us to be one of his DISCIPLES! What an awesome God we serve!

Think about it. Jesus called His 12 disciples with all their issues. They were human. They were self-centered. They didn't get along with most of the others in their group. They often did not fully believe Jesus until He backed up His words with actions (i.e doubting Thomas, the guys in the boat when Jesus calmed the storm, etc.).

The disciples sometimes mistreated people. During the feeding of the 4000/5000, they told Jesus to send them all home without food. Remember how they treated the prostitute who anointed Jesus' feet? One of the disciples was a thief who betrayed Jesus for money. Another one was a zealot, who believed in forced conversions to Judaism. Two of them sent their mom to ask Jesus for a higher place in Heaven among the rest of the group.

They often separated themselves from the group (Simon to Jesus, "Even if the rest of these guys disown you, I won't"). They all took off when the soldiers came to arrest

Jesus, leaving Him by Himself. · Simon (Peter) rejected Jesus three times (even after he just took an oath that he would never do such a thing). Jesus already knew what they would do, but He still called them.

Nothing takes Jesus by surprise, because He is always in control. The psalmist said in Psalm 139 King James Version (KJV) 139 *O Lord, thou hast searched me, and known me. 2 Thou knowest my downsitting and mine uprising, thou understandest my thought afar off. 3 Thou compassest my path and my lying down, and art acquainted with all my ways. 4 For there is not a word in my tongue, but, lo, O Lord, thou knowest it altogether. 5*

Thou hast beset me behind and before and laid thine hand upon me. 6 Such knowledge is too wonderful for me; it is high, I cannot attain unto it. 7 Whither shall I go from thy spirit? or whither shall I flee from thy presence? 8 If I ascend into heaven, thou art there: if I make my bed in hell, behold, thou art there. 9 If I take the wings of the morning and dwell in the uttermost parts of the sea; 10 Even there shall thy hand lead me, and thy right hand shall hold me. 11 If I say, Surely the darkness shall cover me; even the night shall be light about me. 12 Yea, the darkness hideth not from thee; but the night shineth as the day: the darkness and the light are both alike to thee. 13 For thou hast possessed my reins: thou hast covered me in my mother's womb. 14 I will praise thee; for I am fearfully and wonderfully made: marvelous are thy works; and that my soul knoweth right well. 15 My substance was not hidden from thee, when I was made in secret, and curiously wrought in the lowest parts of the earth. 16 Thine eyes did see my substance yet being unperfect; and in thy book all my members were written, which in continuance were fashioned, when yet there was none of them. 17 How precious also are thy thoughts unto me, O God! how great is the sum of them ·

Romans 8:29-30 reminds us that *for whom he did foreknow, he also did predestinate to be conformed to the image of his Son, that he might be the firstborn among many brethren. Moreover, whom he did predestinate, them he also called: and whom he called, them he also justified: and whom he justified, them he also glorified.* God already knew the beginning of our lives to the end. If we could only just trust Him and believe and continue to follow Him and deny our feelings and failures, we could begin to walk in the greatness he called us to.

Just keep moving forward with Him and one day we will hear him say Well done, good and faithful servant. Thou hast been faithful over a few things; I will make thee ruler over many things. Enter thou into the joy of thy Lord.

John 15:16 Says *ye have not chosen me, but I have chosen you, and ordained you, that ye should go and bring forth fruit, and that your fruit should remain: that whatsoever ye shall ask of the Father in my name, he may give it you.* Our destiny for greatness in God has been established from the beginning to the end and throughout eternity. Therefore, you can declare I AM A DISCIPLE and I WIN!!!

We are all destined for greatness. Who told Martin Luther King he would be the greatest? Who told Malcolm X, Lebron James, Michael Jackson, or even Beyoncé that they would be great? Who told Jesus the Christ he would be the savior? They all looked within themselves and found greatness and now you have been equipped to do the same!

List some ways to be Disciplined for greatness

_____

_____

_____

_____

_____

_____

List ways you can be Disciplined affects greatness

_____

_____

I Am A Disciple

_____
_____
_____
_____
_____
_____
_____

What are some benefits of a disciplined

Mind?

_____
_____
_____
_____
_____
_____

What are some issues of an undisciplined
Mind?

_____
_____
_____
_____
_____

What are some steps you can take to
Discipline your Emotions?

_____
_____

_____
_____
_____
_____
_____

What are some problems from having an
undisciplined emotional
makeup:_____
_____
_____
_____
_____
_____
_____

9 I Am Disciplined in my Mind & Emotions

Affirmations:

1:

2:

3:

4:

5:

6:

7:

8:

9:

About the Author

My name is Chris Brown and I am the founder and lead servant of Covenant Purpose & Restoration Family Center. I was born in Dallas; TX, and I grew up in the Baptist and Apostolic faiths. I later moved to Sherman, TX and graduated from Sherman High School. I was called to the ministry at the age of 16 and accepted the call at the age of 18.

I am a licensed Pastor in the World Outreach Christian Assembly and I have ministered in various religious organizations including Missionary Baptist, Full Gospel Holy Temple, Pentecostal

Assemblies of the World, United Pentecostal Church International, African Methodist Episcopal and Church of God in Christ.

I have been the Pastor of Covenant Purpose & Restoration Family Center for 5 years. I am dedicated and have a burden for the lost. At CPR Family Center we focus on holistic ministry by having a food pantry, health and wellness seminars, financial seminars, offering assistance with Medicaid and Medicare sign up, feeding the homeless, and focus on outreach in the Medical District of Dallas, TX. I am joined by our Co-Pastor and lovely wife of 15 years, April Brown who fervently serves with me in the ministry. We

are a growing ministry and will continue to do the work that God has set before us and change the lives of those in our community and the world!